Wishfilled Thinking

by
Professer Klunk

Illustrated by
Richard Stack

Published by

**DOWN THE PATH
PUBLISHING**

First Edition
Published in Canada 2009
By Down the Path Publishing
PO Box 344, Clearwater B.C. V0E 1N0

Email: David@DavidVanstone.com

Library and Archives Canada Cataloguing in Publication

Klunk, Clickity 1955-
Wishfilled thinking / by Clickity Klunk; illustrated by Richard Stack.

(A cautionary tale by Professer Klunk)
Also issued in mini softcover format.
ISBN 978-0-9689899-7-5

I. Stack, Richard, 1946- II. Title.
III. Series: Klunk, Clickity, 1955- . Cautionary tale.

PS8621.L856W58 2009 jC813'.6 C2009-904719-5

ISBN 978-0-9689899-7-5

PRINTED IN CHINA

Wishfilled Thinking

Now this is a story

About a tree, who thought,

"I sure would live longer

If I was a rock."

So he rented scary movies

About a man with an axe.

The chainsaw chipping thriller

Made his sap thicken fast.

He felt pretty scared
But nowhere inside
Did it go past being scared
Nowhere near petrified.

Every fall he'd take leave,
Take leave go to sleep,
Dreaming of how rocks
Existence they keep.

Yet spring after spring
He would wake up a tree
And wish to a rock
He'd transform to be.

Then one day the earth
Quaked at his place,
Tumbling the tree down
Down the rock face.

Buried beneath hundreds,

Thousands of tons of rubble,

The conditions were right

The transformation was subtle.

Many years later

Again the ground it did shift,

Giving this once upon tree

An upwardly lift.

Back on the surface

Came this petrified wood,

Not quite as a rock but

As best as he could.

So ends this story

As we both here do see ~

Wishes can come nearly true

As they did for that tree.

About the Artist

Richard Stack showed promise as an artist as early as Grade school – his first piece of art was published in a newsletter in North West Territories in the mid-50s.

In London, Ontario, Richard studied architectural drafting and rendering. The Winnipeg Art Gallery was his place of study for two years in the early 60s followed by a Commercial Art Diploma at Red River Community College.

PHOTO BY HAZEL STACK

When and wherever Richard travels he takes the time to learn about and from the local art and takes many pictures for future paintings.

Besides illustrations Richard spends time creating works of art using watercolours, acrylic paint and airbrush.

Living seaside his creativity has extended to include woodcarvings of dolphins, whales and birds ~ frequently using driftwood found locally. People in Canada, USA, Asia, India and Africa share his works of art.

Richard is pleased to be asked by Professer Klunk to illustrate this book.

Proofread by Leslie Schlack and Ruth Caspell
Desktop Publishing by Linda Mullin
e-mail Linda@mullinart.com

Other Books by Professer Clickity Klunk

A Puppy Named Rufus
A Puppy Named Rufus Mini

Horace the Cat
Horace the Cat Mini

Wishfilled Thinking Mini

DOWN THE PATH PUBLISHING

PO Box 344
Clearwater, BC
V0E 1N0

e-mail: Books@ProfesserKlunk.com